Adventures in Cartooning

James Sturm
Andrew Arnold
Alexis Frederick-Frost

SCHOLASTIC INC.
New York Toronto London Auckland
Sydney Mexico City New Delhi Hong Kong

For Eva and Charlotte
-JS

For Mom and Dad
-AA

For Grandma, Leslie, Mom and Dad
-AFF

Once upon a time... a princess tried to make a comic...

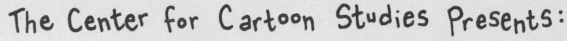

TURES
CARTOONING

HOW DOODLES BECOME STORIES

Ta-daaaah!!!

AND A **MAGICAL** ELF!

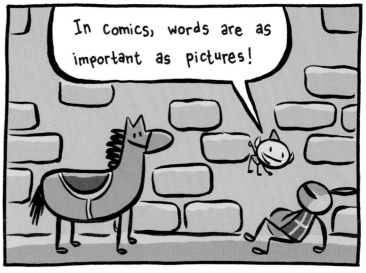

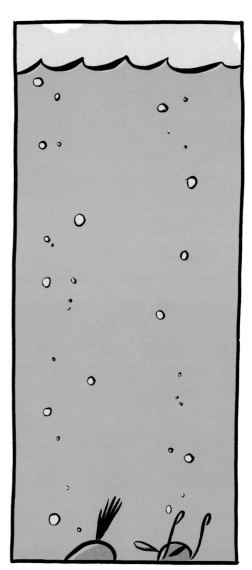

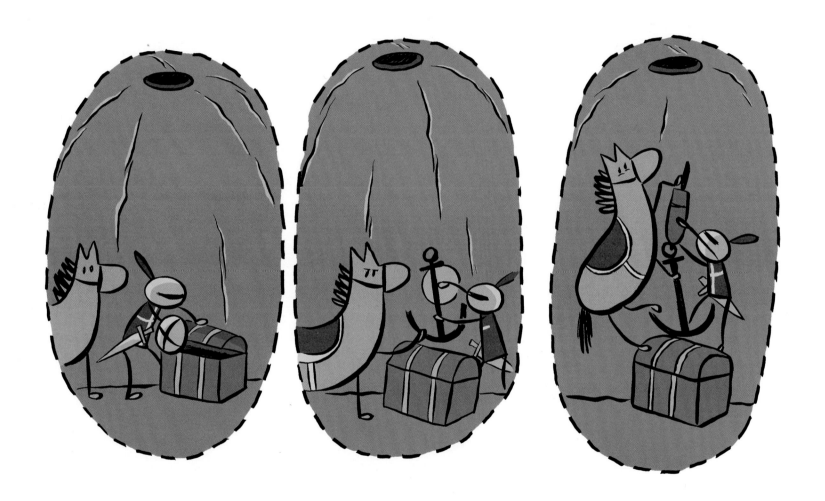

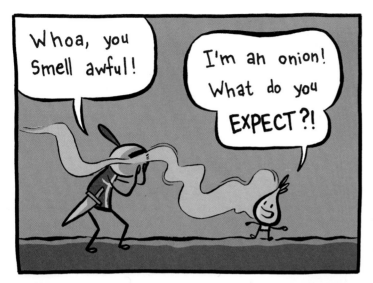

78

HELLO!

The Elf!

Wow, that was a great adventure! I loved how you put those word balloons together!

Gasp

And that giant two-page panel!

A real show-stopper!

And the knight was the princess! I guess she wanted to be part of the adventure and not just be shown how to do it!

Hey! Where did everybody go?!

THE END

 BONUS FEATURE!

The MAGICAL ELF'S
Cartooning Basics

Will this be on a test?!!!

Panel:
- Where your drawings go
- A MOMENT IN TIME!

Gutter:
The space between panels

Tier:
One row of panels

Word Balloon:
When someone talks, the words go in here.

Stem:
Points to whoever is talking.

Thought Balloon:
When someone is thinking, the words go in here!

The stems are bubbles!

Word balloons can have different shapes depending on what's being said:

EXCITED!

SCREAMING!

102

Advanced cartooning tips starring **Edward!**

A scribble above head shows frustration

Lines show excitement or a burst of energy!!!

Z s show sleep or tiredness...

Sweat drops for nervousness or sadness

Drops for drool! Hungry!!!

Boo!

Lines for suprise!

Little bubbles for tired or woozy!

Lines for action and movement!

This book grew out of an assignment given by James Sturm at the Center for Cartoon Studies in White River Junction, VT using Ed Emberly's book, **Make a World**, as inspiration. Alexis Frederick-Frost and Andrew Arnold were students in the school's very first class! Thanks, Ed Emberly!

For more information on the Center for Cartoon Studies, visit www.cartoonstudies.org

The knight

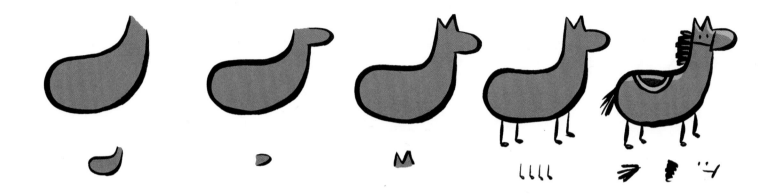

Edward

Elf

Ok! Now **YOU** try drawing a story! Grab some paper and a pencil or pen !!!

Here's a great example of how to do it!

A Fishy Story

BY Eva

ABOUT THE
AUTHORS

STARRING

The Elf's
EVIL
TWIN,
DOCTOR
INKENSTAIN

My **brother** thinks he knows **so** much about comics.

But I'll show him. I'll make a comic that PROVES I am the greatest!!!

Here, in my lab a hundred feet below the dragon's volcano, I have used **mad science** to create:

A CARTOONING MONSTER!

Do I know you two?

Remember, James, I'm Andrew.

And I'm Alexis.

ISBN 978-0-545-24965-2

12 11 10 9 8 7   17 18 19/0

                                                                         40

Printed in the U.S.A.

First Scholastic printing, March 2010